HALF-CRACKED

HALF-CRACKED
THE LEGEND OF SISSY MARY

MARY-COLIN CHISHOLM

Playwrights Canada Press
Toronto

Playwrights Canada Press
202-269 Richmond St. w., Toronto, ON M5V 1X1
416.703.0013 | info@playwrightscanada.com | www.playwrightscanada.com

LIBRARY AND ARCHIVES CANADA CATALOGUING IN PUBLICATION
Title: Half-cracked : the legend of Sissy Mary / Mary-Colin Chisholm.
Names: Chisholm, Mary-Colin, author.
Description: First edition. | A play.
Identifiers: Canadiana (print) 20230183670 | Canadiana (ebook) 20230183778
| ISBN 9780369104069 (softcover) | ISBN 9780369104076 (EPUB)
| ISBN 9780369104083 (PDF)
Classification: LCC PS8605.H73575 H35 2023 | DDC C812/.6—dc23

Playwrights Canada Press operates on land which is the current and ancestral home of the Anishinaabe Nations (Ojibwe / Chippewa, Odawa, Potawatomi, Algonquin, Saulteaux, Nipissing, and Mississauga), the Wendat, and the members of the Haudenosaunee Confederacy (Mohawk, Oneida, Onondaga, Cayuga, Seneca, and Tuscarora), as well as Metis and Inuit peoples. It always was and always will be Indigenous land.

We acknowledge the financial support of the Canada Council for the Arts, the Ontario Arts Council (OAC), Ontario Creates, and the Government of Canada for our publishing activities.

Canada Council for the Arts   Conseil des arts du Canada

ONTARIO ARTS COUNCIL
CONSEIL DES ARTS DE L'ONTARIO
an Ontario government agency
un organisme du gouvernement de l'Ontario

Canada

ONTARIO CREATES | ONTARIO CRÉATIF

To my siblings, Corinne Cameron and Chris Chisholm,
two great storytellers. Thanks for all my best lines.

And to the jerks in junior high who nicknamed me
"Hen." Thanks for the resilience.

"If we had a keen vision and feeling of all ordinary human life, it would be like hearing the grass grow and the squirrel's heart beat, and we should die of that roar which lies on the other side of silence."

—George Eliot, *Middlemarch*

"All babies are beautiful, especially the homely ones."

—Kathryn "Danny Kirk" Chisholm

First presented as *Sugar Mary & Yewina* in a staged workshop by LunaSea Theatre in Kjipuktuk, Mi'kma'ki. It was presented at KAZAN CO-OP's Waiting Room, Agricola Street, Halifax, 2016, with the following cast and creative team:

Sugar Mary: Margaret Smith
Yewina: Mary-Colin Chisholm
Scott: Christian Murray

Director: Martha Irving
Dramaturge: Jackie Torrens
Stage Manager and Choreographer: Ryanne Chisholm

The second staged reading was at Eastern Front Theatre's 2016 STAGES Theatre Festival, at Deep Water Church, with the following cast and creative team:

Sugar Mary: Margaret Smith
Yewina: Ryanne Chisholm
Scott: Christian Murray

Director: Martha Irving
Choreographer: Ryanne Chisholm
Production Manager: Gina Thornhill

The world premiere was on March 13, 2018, at Neptune Theatre's Scotiabank Stage, Argyle Street, Halifax, as *Half-Cracked: The Legend of Sugar Mary*. It was a co-production between Neptune Theatre and Eastern Front Theatre with the following cast and creative team:

Sugar Mary: Geneviève Steele
Yewina: Sharleen Kalayil
Scott: Christian Murray

Director: Martha Irving
Assistant Director: Jacob Planinc
Stage Manager: Ingrid Risk
Set Design and Painting: Holly Carr
Technical Assistance and Builder: Garrett Barker
Sound Design: June Zinck
Lighting Design: Ingrid Risk

Author's Notes

Sissy and Yewina are not blood relatives. If they are of different ethnicity, when Sissy is wondering if "Daddy" or "Mom" had her after an affair, Yewina can reference the wedding photo and add an "Uh, not likely." Scott has slight Indigenous ancestry, but no lived experience or recognized nation affiliation. He would see himself as a generic American. When Scott talks about his parents the text can be tweaked to fit the actor, e.g., "My mother is half-Norwegian, half-Nigerian." Or, "My dad came to Arizona State on a full golf scholarship from Bangalore." His background can be unlikely—the whole play is unlikely.

The dialogue is partially written colloquially, e.g., "whaddya" for "what do you." It's meant to be a general nudge in the direction of my eastern Nova Scotia roots. Please don't be religious about it. Sissy's word mangles aren't consistent but that's just her. When people speak simultaneously, I've put them on the same line. I've indicated overlaps with the slanted line (/). Ellipses (. . .) can signify trailing off or switching thoughts. Dashes (—) are cut-offs. It's not an exact science. You can use or lose f-bombs as you like, or as your audience tolerates. You can substitute f-bombs with friggin', frackin', gee dee, jeezly, etc. "Beag" is pronounced bek, and is Gaelic for little. "Mor" is pronounced more and means big. "Yup" can be spoken on an inhale.

Sissy Mary and Yewina's house is cheery, full of odd bits and bobs and not terribly tidy with lots of spiderwebs. There's a cot (or sofa) by the stove, with old quilts and pillows. Nothing is newer than thirty years. It lives in current time and yet in its own time and timelessness.

Some objects that are used or referenced include:

Wildflower bouquets
Old, light rifle—break action if possible—and a box of birdshot shells
Dead rabbit in a sack, and a few groceries
Skinning knife
Money and "Rainy Day Fund" sugar bowl
Spiderwebs
Playing cards
Kettle, tea and coffee pot, canned milk, cups and dishes, dish cloths, etc.
Cookies and jar
Rotary phone
Tool box with tools and an old letter
Scott's kit bag and small tape recorder (or cellphone)
Eggs in shell, speckly
Vintage lady's shoe with tissue
Scott's pen, notebook, cellphone
Sprig of dried bayberry
Portable record player and a few records
Christmas card in French
Tweezers, pellets on tin plate
Six books including: *The Norton Anthology of English Literature,
Northanger Abbey, Riders of the Purple Sage, The Secret of the Old Clock*
Fresh corpses of Sheila the Hen and John Arthur Rooster

Through a window we may (or may not) see part of the henhouse. An old
ladder is used to block the henhouse door to keep the hens safe at night.
Scott moves it to an upright position to climb on to the roof—the play has
been done without us seeing it.

Some part of the set signifies an apple tree. The set can be literal and/or poetic.

Sissy and Yewina have been on their own, who knows how long exactly.
They're a bit vague on dates and facts. Their rural community has been
losing residents for years. No more lobster canning factory, no more
gypsum mining, no more sheep and beef farming, no more young families
with tons of kids . . . Just the two sisters, some miles from town, in a
weathered farmhouse, in a place that used to be.

Dramatis personae

Sissy Mary: female-presenting
Yewina: female-presenting
Scott: male-presenting

The relative relationships are more important than the ages. Sissy has to be younger than Yewina. Yewina has to be old enough to have tried university a while ago. Scott is old enough have wandered and squandered some time. He can be about the same age as Sissy or younger.

Act One

Prologue

Twilight. Apple tree. SISSY is chasing Sheila, her chicken (real, puppet, or mime—yer pick). Sheila clucks conversationally, squawks and flaps as needed.

SISSY: Here, chickachickachicka, here, Sheila, ha—there you are! C'mon, Sheila, it's getting dark, what are you doing in that apple tree again? You can't be roosting out here. You gotta go in with John Arthur and the girls—d'ya want the fox or the weasel or . . . the coggar to get you?

Squawk!

All right, shush now, I'll tell you a story . . .

Sheila flutters down and allows SISSY to hold her.

Hmm, what'll it be . . . oh how about the time Marcella Brophy and the lost child—?

Cluck.

No? How about . . . the ghost fire ship at Malignant Cove?

Cluck.

. . . I thought you liked—?

Cluck.

Nope? Okay . . . the Haunted Fish Truck of Isle a Haute?

A long squawk.

I know there's no fish trucks on Isle a Haute—that's the weird part!

Cluck.

Gosh maybe I'm running out of stories . . . oh, how about the time Francis Bouchie caught the Sea-Hag—

A "maybe" cluck.

Yeah that's a good'un. Francis was hauling lobster traps, tugging and hauling and he thought "what in the hell is that coming outta the water?" It looked like a big knot of red kelp, but oh my god, wasn't it was a mess of ugly old red hair on top of an ugly old Sea Hag! She was setting on his trap and she reached up and—ach.

Sheila is squirmy.

Oh my jeez but you're restless. Why're ya so fridgety? . . . I am too. There's something in the air. What is it I wonder . . . ? It feels like . . . like this one other time—I was soaked after a thundrelstorm on Mackie point with a double rainbow I felt . . . And I'm feeling that again . . . Hm. Here.

She lies down with Sheila.

This is what we'll do. Lie here and let your eyes go softlike, don't look at what you're looking at and then you can see the world as a big circle . . . see? Like we're in the middle of everything and the world is a big circle holding us . . .

She demonstrates peripheral vision.

Tommy Day showed me how to see things like this once, when I came up from the beach and there was Tommy lying in the scratchy beach grass on top of the dune and he sat up and he smiled and he said, "You can see the sky better if you don't look at it." And he showed me how to lay down so the beach grass didn't hurt and how to make my eyes go so I could see the whole rim of the world and I did and I felt myself float up and I just felt so . . .

Sheila doesn't get this and clucks grumpily.

Oh all right, never mind, maybe chicken eyes are difdrent. C'mon, it's getting late and I want to make those cookies Yewina likes—

Cluck?

Because she's my sister and sisters gotta take care of sisters, right? And you got to get to bed so you and the girls can make eggs for Yewina to take to town tomorrow.

Clucking and music shift to . . .

Scene One

Next day, afternoon. In the kitchen.

YEW: Thanks now, Dan!

> *Holding a light shotgun and a gunny sack, she waves through the door or fourth wall to Dan's unseen postal van. A horn "toot-toots" as he pulls out. SISSY comes running in to wave bye.*

SISSY: Bye Dan!

> *SISSY waves enthusiastically as the van disappears. When she can no longer see it, she turns to YEWINA.*

All of them?

YEW: Yup, coulda sold twice as many.

> *YEW puts her gun against the wall and pulls a dead rabbit from the sack putting it in the sink. She gets money out of her pocket.*

There's for the Rainy Day Fund.

SISSY: Oooh!

> *SISSY happily counts the money and tucks it in the sugar bowl. As YEW gets a deck of cards off a shelf, a spiderweb sticks to her fingers.*

YEW: Aach. *(sarcastic)* What d'ya say, Sissy, think we got enough spiderwebs in this house?

SISSY: *(considers seriously)* Hm … yeah … Yeah, I think so.

> *YEW sighs.*

Who'd you see in town?

YEW: Oh, Jerry Jones.

SISSY: Jerry Gerald? Jerry Jerome?

YEW: Jerry Gerard.

SISSY: Euw. What was he saying?

YEW: Not much.

SISSY: How's their mother?

YEW: Ah, she's walking again.

SISSY: Yup, eggs'll put the strength back in ya—you made sure Agnes got the speckley brown ones.

YEW: Huh.

SISSY: Yewina! You make sure she gets Sheila's eggs!

YEW: An egg's an egg.

SISSY: Sheila's eggs are the best! You have to—

YEW: I did, I did, luvvagod, Sissy, I gave her the brown speckled ones.

SISSY: Good 'cause Agnes'll be just like her mother—Mrs. Willie Hector didn't go in the ground until she was a hundred and two. And she had an egg a day. Eggs are rejubvilnating.

YEW: Rejuvenating.

YEW corrects SISSY's mispronunciations reflexively and without expectation, it's an old futile habit.

SISSY: They're restorkative.

YEW: Restorative. Agnes'll never go as long as she's waiting hand and foot on them three Jerrys.

SISSY: She should never have moved them to town. I wish they'd come back and visit sometime . . . I wish somebody would visit.

YEW: They're all too busy.

SISSY: With what?

YEW: Busy being busy.

SISSY: That's foolish, busy being busy? If there's nothing to do, then that's what you should be doing.

YEW: Ayup.

SISSY: I was thinking I got to hold a few eggs back for Sheila to hatch new chicks. But I'll wait until Agnes is all better, can't cut her off now.

YEW: *(wryly)* No, the shock'd kill her.

SISSY: Yeah, the shock'd—hm.

    SISSY almost wonders if YEW is being sarcastic.

I don't know what's got into Sheila. She's after sneaking off and roosting in the apple tree when it's time to go in the henhouse for the night. I don't want the coggar getting—

YEW: There's no more coggar—

SISSY: I seen the end of his tail last fall, whipping by the corner of the old barn.

YEW sighs.

YEW: All right . . . Supper's in the sink.

SISSY: What? Ah no, that darn twisty road again?

YEW: Yeah, jumped right out at us.

SISSY takes a dead rabbit out of the sink.

SISSY: Ah, dear little bunny—ooh nice and meaty, tho'!

YEW starts playing solitaire while SISSY hangs, skins, and cleans the rabbit. She either mimes this or does it just slightly out of view of our potentially squeamish audience.

Who else you see? Yewina? Who else? Yewina? Yewina? Yewina? 'Weena? 'Weenaweenaweenaweenawee—?

YEW: Nobody.

SISSY: Nobody?

YEW: Nope.

SISSY: Who bought eggs then?

YEW: Ohhhhhhhhhh. Cliffie Pettipas.

SISSY: Still looking over his shoulder?

YEW: Yup.

SISSY: Who else?

YEW: Ahhhhhhhhhh. The hippies.

SISSY: Zephania and Windhawk? Aww, I remember when they came here, 'member—the purple school bus?

YEW: Yup.

SISSY: Living in that big tent on the old MacKenzie property, back of beyond, remember?

YEW: Oh yup.

SISSY: And 'member Windhawk having the baby in the blizzard, in the middle of the night and the tent collapsed and Zephania made it to our place and Daddy had to harness up Delmar to dig her out and get her to the hopspital, 'member?

At some point in all this, SISSY comes out with bloody hands.

YEW: Last baby born here.

SISSY: Baby Ziggy. What's he doing now?

YEW: In Europe, studying to be a clown.

SISSY: Well he was born in a tent. I like hippies, though. Always something difdrent. We should have them out for supper.

YEW snorts.

What.

YEW: Nothing.

SISSY: You say hello to Windhawk next time from me.

YEW: She goes by Kimberly now and I will.

SISSY: *(absently, playing with the sounds)* Kimmm berrrrr leee . . .

> *YEW plays her solitaire game.* SISSY *is feeling the electricity in the air.*

What's it like, Yewina?

YEW: What's what like?

SISSY: You know, doing . . . making . . . having—

YEW: What?

SISSY: Sex!

YEW: What in the hell?

SISSY: When you went with Mike Dunagan, didn't you do it?

YEW: Jeezismary'njoseph. What's with you?

SISSY: He had awful pretty hair.

YEW: Yeah, I should've skinned him for his pelt and left the rest of him for the crows.

SISSY: Ahh. Didn't you like him?

YEW: Yeah.

SISSY: So?

YEW: So what?

SISSY: I know you guys did it that summer before you went to college, 'member the night at the Maryvale Dance, after Mike knocked out Vincie MacVicar for grabbing you.

YEW: Hey, it was me who knocked out Vincie MacVicar.

SISSY: Really?

YEW: He was grabbing my arse and I spun around and pucked him one. Put him down quick.

SISSY: Well, here I always thought it was Mike floored Vincie. That's too bad.

YEW: Why is that too bad?

SISSY: Because it would have been more romantic if Mike had a done it. Protecting your honour. You know. Shrivaldry.

YEW: Chivalry. Like Mike had any of that. I skinned my knuckles on Vincie's crooked front tooth, protecting me own arse and honour, thank you very much.

SISSY: Oh yes, Vincie had those awful rat teeth. See that's probably why he was after grabbing your arse, those rat teeth. Poor Vincie. Ah, what a sin. I thought that's maybe why you went with Mike . . .

YEW: Maybe it was.

SISSY: Wha'?

YEW: Look. I don't know if it counts as romantic or not but it was kind of . . . exciting, I guess. Mike looked at me like he couldn't believe his eyes and I said, "Well, do I got to slug you too?" and he got all googley and "wha'wha'wha'??" and I just said "Well, do want to or not?" And he said, "yeah" and we hauled it back to the truck and . . . that was that.

SISSY: That was that?

YEW: That was that.

SISSY: Hm.

    Pause.

Didn't you want to see each other again?

YEW: We were going to but—that was that—because Ethel told me Mike went and got Donna Dumphy up the stump pregnant at the Catholic Youth Lenten retreat.

SISSY: Wow . . . tsk, and they had all those freckly kids.

YEW: Ten. Ten freckly mouth breathers.

SISSY: Aww, cute though. Just think, 'Weena, if you'd been on that Lenten retreat, you might be the one living over top the dry cleaners right now with Mike Dunagan and ten kids!

YEW: Eeew. Why are you bringin' this up now?

SISSY: I was telling Sheila about when Tommy Day showed me how to see the world like a bowl / and how—

YEW: / What brought that on?

SISSY: Don't you feel it? In the air? Something itching to happen!

YEW: Oh my god.

SISSY: And Sheila feels it—

YEW: Am I gonna have to take you to Doc MacMaster again . . . ?

SISSY: No.

YEW: Good. I hope not.

SISSY: Never mind, you don't get it . . . I wonder if I should pull some carrots to go with that rabbit. Ah, hahaha—get it, carrots with the rabbit?

    Sharp inhale as she sees the cards.

Ooooo . . .

YEW: Hey now.

SISSY: Jack and nine.

YEW: Sissy!

SISSY: Hearts and spades.

YEW: Stop it.

SISSY: With the stranger comes a danger.

YEW: Go put the tea on.

SISSY: Whhew.

    Another sharp inhale from SISSY.

YEW: Fertheluvva.

SISSY: —four shovels—the Spinster! —what's this crossing her?

    YEW *gathers up the cards.*

YEW: All right, frig off.

SISSY: The big heart and the one eye.

YEW: I'll put the tea on.

SISSY: You should put enough water in the kettle for three.

YEW: Oh just, f—just, you—stop with that! You're not some magic, witchy whatever. All right?

Suddenly, a knock at the door. Lights down.

Scene Two

Lights up. Later. The table has three cups on it and the remnants of a rabbit stew meal. SCOTT is self-consciously finishing his tea.

SCOTT: Well.

SISSY pours more tea.

Thank you, Sissy Mary. That was a real nice stew.

YEW: Fresh rabbit, nice and fat on summer berries.

SCOTT: You betcha, Miss Yewina, thank you. But I really should call the garage if you have a pho—

YEW: What's your name, again?

SCOTT: Wow, did I not introduce myself? I'm so sorry, where are my manners? My name is / Scott,

SISSY: / Scott—

YEW: Scott. Why're you called Scott?

SCOTT: Guess my mum just liked the name.

SISSY: *(softly, hovering, staring at him)* Ssssc . . . ot.

YEW: Where you from, Scott?

SCOTT: Scottsdale. Scottsdale, Arizona.

YEW: Scott from Scottsdale. Family still there?

SCOTT: My brother, Dale. And my folks yeah . . .

SISSY: Ssssc . . . ot . . .

YEW: So. You're Scottish, Scott?

SCOTT: No—I don't really know, maybe somewhere back there—

YEW: You don't know?

SCOTT: I'm kind of a Heinz 57. My mum's half-Norwegian, and my father is maybe some Irish or German—that's the Heinz part.

> *SISSY laughs.*

SISSY: Ketchup.

SCOTT: Yeah, a bit of everything—actually, my grandfather is part . . . Cherokee? I think.

SISSY: Wow.

SCOTT: I think . . . We never talked much about it . . .

YEW: What do you talk about?

SCOTT: Ah . . . Golf.

YEW: Golf.

SCOTT: My folks run a golf store and golf school.

YEW: Golfing.

SCOTT: The Duffer's Hut 'n Putt and Elite Eagle Golf Academy. My folks met on the golf course. My brother's a pro golfer. Yup. Big on golf.

> *YEW and SISSY stare.*

Lotsa . . . golf. Either of you golf?

> *YEW and SISSY stare and slowly shake their head, no. Pause.*

SISSY: I was a sugar tit baby.

YEW: Sissy . . .

SCOTT: Sugar t—sorry?

SISSY: Sugar tit baby. Daddy found me in the barn and—

SCOTT: In the barn—?

YEW: First frame truss barn built on this road. Falling down now—

SISSY: But I'm still here.

YEW: Roof needs work.

SISSY: I was a brand new, newborned baby.

YEW: Cheap nails, last time it was done—

SISSY: Nobody ever knew where I come from—

YEW: —rotted the cedar shakes.

SISSY: —some poor girl had me and she set me in the straw—

YEW: —Yup, big job, that roof.

SISSY: —so that she could go to the convent in Halifax and start life anew with the nuns and then go to Hollywood to make inspirnaytional fillums because of her great beauty and because she understood tragedy.

YEW: Cripes. Yeah, Daddy comes in one day and goes, "Well, you'll never guess what I found in the barn."

SISSY: And Yewina said—

YEW: A puppy?   **SISSY:** A puppy!

YEW: Always wanted a puppy.

SISSY: I coulda been a puppy. I only weighed two pounds and I woulda died if the Black Hen hadn't been brooding on me. She kept me warm because I had no clothes oh, but I did have my caul.

SCOTT: Caul?

SISSY: Want to s—?

YEW: Leave it, Sissy.

SISSY: I can show you later.

YEW: He don't care about cauls.

SCOTT: Oh caul! C-A-U-L. Actually I've read a bit about cauls, or birth veils. If I remember rightly, they have significance in West African cultures uh, Ashanti, Yoruba, so forth and of course they figure in Druidic systems / as well.

SISSY: / droolidic . . .

SCOTT: Dru—yeah.

SISSY: Is it the same as here? When miracle babies are born they come with a piece of skin like a little French beret settin' on their heads.

SCOTT: Yes, the amniotic sac—that's the birth membrane.

SISSY: Ah. It's a caul. I can show you later. I still got it in the attic with the baptizzle papers—

YEW: Baptism. Don't be draggin' that friggin' caul / out.

SISSY: / I got it wrapped up in tissue and saved in the toe of Mom's wedding shoe.

YEW: Later.

SISSY: Later. I said that, Yewina, later. I can show you later. When Daddy found me just like that tucked in the straw, with the Black Hen, here's the miracle; the chickens never pecked me, not one peck. They respected the caul.

YEW: Blah.

SISSY: What?

YEW: Chickens will kill their own and you think they respected your caul?

SISSY: Chickens are creatures of god—they seen I was blessed and meant to be.

YEW: Jeesis, Sissy, of course you were meant to be—everything's meant to be—shit, flies are meant to be but that don't keep a chicken from pecking the shit out of a shit fly!

SISSY: So how do you explain them chickens never pecking me?

YEW: You freaked them out.

SISSY: I was cute.

YEW: With your gaddam caul.

SISSY: She's teasing. I was cute. Daddy said I was as cute as all get out.

YEW: You weren't no puppy.

SISSY: I was a miracle. 'Cause I had a caul. But poor Mom, she didn't see it like that at first, hey. When Daddy brung me in, straw hanging off me and my caul still on like a jaunty French beret.

YEW: Oh my god.

SISSY: She passed out, boom, down like a stunned calf, woke up screeching.

YEW: Okay, enough of that.

SISSY: She didn't want nothin' to do with me at first see—but that was just at first—

YEW: —Arizona! How's the weather out there?

SCOTT: Hot.

YEW: Hot?

SISSY: —Same day I was found, Mary May Mosey came by selling bakskets and she showed Daddy how to put some sugar and warm water on a rag see—a sugar tit!

YEW: Cripes.

SISSY: And I sucked on that for three days and by then they'd found me a nanny goat—aww Nanny!

YEW: Yup, anyway—

SISSY: And at first I was that damn "Sugar Tit Baby" and then just "Sugar" for a while, but Yewina always wanted a little sister.

YEW: No I never.

SISSY: So she called me Sissy

YEW: No I never.

SISSY: Yes you did and then—

YEW: I wanted a puppy.

SISSY: And then when they baptizzeled me—

YEW: —Baptised.

SISSY: —they made me "Sissy Mary," so it would be more Christian on the cer-tifleclit—

YEW: —Certificate.

SISSY: —and I'm also called Mary, a little bit after the Virgin Mary and a little bit after Mary May Mosey. See that baksket there? She made that, that's what I slept in.

SCOTT: Wow.

SISSY: Chickens still love me.

YEW: We shoulda called you Barnie.

SISSY: Not funny, Yewina.

YEW: Found ya in a barn.

SISSY: Barnie is a boy's name, not funny. Do you want to see my caul now?

YEW: What year's your Volvo?

SCOTT: Ah, '94.

YEW: '94.   **SISSY:** I'll go get it.

YEW: He doesn't care about your stinky old caul!

SCOTT: No, no—I'm very interested, although, as you say maybe later. This is the kind of ah, colloquial history—colloquial meaning "informally spoken"—that is important to document.

SISSY: Plus it's true, it's my story.

YEW: Hm. What are you doing here anyways, Scott?

SCOTT: I'm researching for a project in folkloric studies towards a possible master's.

YEW: Oh yeah?

SCOTT: The working title is— "Orts and Scraps: Remnants and detritus of obsolete folklore in an erased community." Ort is an archaic word—archaic meaning "old"—an old word for scrap—

SISSY: —why don't you call it "Scraps and Scraps"?

SCOTT: Because it's "Orts and Scraps."

YEW: Remnants and—?   **SISSY:** ... Or "Orts and Orts."

SCOTT: Detritus—from the Latin, what's left / behind—

SISSY: / because they mean the same / thing

YEW: / So, remnant—same thing as detritus, same thing as ort, same thing as scraps—?

SISSY: / Ooooorrrrr—t / ssss

SCOTT: / The title's still a work in progress.

SISSY: Or just / "Orts" or just / "Scraps" because if an ort is a scrap and a scrap is a remnant and a remnant is a ditteris destra ditsa Detroit uterus . . . *(overlap naturally, find your rhythm)*

YEW: / they all mean the same right, like an ort is a remnant, right? Or maybe like, is an ort an old scrap? 'Cause if detritus is a remnant—?

SCOTT: / Yeah, ah yeah . . . Okay— Yeah! *(overlapping stops)* Well like I say, the title's not totally decided. I'll think about your . . . suggestions, thanks. Anyhow, I'm on a grant through the college's Folklore and Ethnology Department to interview community elders, specifically on local legends. Nobody's ever recorded anything from this part of the world—but I found an old letter in the department files from a Dr. MacMaster—?

SISSY: He's about a mile past us. But . . .

YEW: You wouldn't get much of him now. Hardening of the arteries.

SISSY: He hasn't been the same since Ethel—

YEW: Shst!

SISSY: —since the tw—

YEW: Shst!

SISSY: —since, the little? people left.

YEW: Gaddamn it.

SCOTT: The little—?

YEW: They're gone! All right. Nobody knows where.

SCOTT: All right. I understand Dr. MacMaster practised medicine here for over sixty years?

YEW: That's right. He's not from here.

SCOTT: Unfortunately, because the letter was misfiled, no one ever contacted him from the university, but at that time he said he had stories he wished to have recorded, stories gleaned through his practice treating the local characters—

SISSY & YEW: Characters?

YEW: Anyway, I don't think your rig's gonna take you there.

SCOTT: No I guess not. Gosh then, I guess a lift to town would be the thing.

YEW: Too bad Delmar's gone.

SISSY: Aww, Delmar.

SCOTT: Delmar?

YEW: Our old horse. And we don't have a car anymore. We get in and out with Dan, the mailman.

SISSY: That's right, Yewina rides shotgun into town to sell our eggs.

SCOTT: And how would I contact Dan for—

YEW: S'Friday night. He won't be going by again until Monday.

SCOTT: So okay, boy, if I hear you right, we are pretty isolated. Neighbours?

SISSY: Clifford Pettipas, where you turn in.

SCOTT: I didn't see a house.

YEW: No. He burnt it down.

SISSY: To get away from the Devil.

SCOTT: Oh?

SISSY: The Devil used to chase him all around the old house. So he burnt it down and moved into town, into a new house on Church Street. But it didn't work out too good though, right, 'Weena?

YEW: Yeah, he told me, "The thing of it is, the old place was nice and big with all kinds of hidey spots but this here bungalow's too damn small. Now, the Devil's after catching me all the time now."

SISSY: Poor Cliffie. What a sin, hey?

SCOTT: Yeah. So, no other neighbours.

SISSY: Lots. The Jerry Joneses, the Brophys, the—

YEW: All gone.

SISSY: Yup. Dead, moved, or . . . gone. Everybody wants to live in town.

YEW: People don't like driving this road, you gotta cross over that old bridge, bad turns, blind hills . . .

SCOTT: Maybe I could call a garage? If I could use your ph—

SISSY: And a lotta roadkill. Did you hit anything?

SCOTT: No, it wasn't that. Just lost all power on that last incline. Then I saw your driveway. So, do you have a ph—

SISSY: Dan hit a rabbit today. But almost every other day it's something, rabbit, partridge, porcupine, right, Yewina?

YEW nods.

—twice he hit a pig

SCOTT: Sorry?

YEW: Yeah, yeah that's uh, yeah some people hey? Letting their pigs run loose like that. Tsk, tsk, tsk.

SISSY: Dan is terrible for hitting animals with that big postal van and then it's up to Yewina to put them out of their misery.

YEW: Ahyup.

SISSY: It's a hard world for little things. And pigs. Be a shame to waste the meat though.

YEW: Yup. That's—yup.

SCOTT: I see . . . Um, do you have a phone . . . ?

A phone sits in plain view.

SISSY & YEW: Yup.

SCOTT: May I use it?

SISSY & YEW: Doesn't work.

SCOTT: Okay. This is tricky. I can't get any bars on my cell out here.

YEW: Oh you can. If you go on top of the henhouse—that's what the fellah from Lands and Forests did.

SISSY: Yup, from when I reported the coggar.

YEW: Gahgk.

SCOTT: Sorry?

SISSY: Yewina doesn't believe me but I seen him, the ol' coggar himself, last fall.

YEW: Cougar. Eastern Cougar. Extinct.

SISSY: Yeah "stinct."

> *SISSY rolls her eyes.*

I'll show you the ladder. C'mon.

SCOTT: I don't think I've ever been on top of a henhouse . . .

SISSY: C'mon.

> *SISSY takes him out towards the henhouse. Some of the outdoor action may be visible through the kitchen window. YEW, alone in the kitchen, gets out an old tool box.*

(*off stage*) You take off the ladder that's holding the door shut and prop 'er up. Just make sure you put it back acrost the door when you're done. If John Arthur comes at ya—swat him.

SCOTT: (*off stage*) John Ar—?

SISSY: (*off stage*) The rooster, if comes he at ya.

SCOTT: (*off stage*) Thank you, this is great.

> *He climbs up and away.*

YEW: *(addressing the tool box)* Don't worry, Daddy, I got my eye on her . . .

> *YEW is checking the tools in the box as SISSY drifts back into the kitchen. SISSY watches out the window transfixed.*

Sissy, I'm going to go and have a look under the hood.

SISSY: Of all the hills on all the roads, in all the world, he lost power on our hill and coasted into our driveway.

YEW: Yeah . . .

SISSY: Of all the driveways, on all the hills . . .

> *YEW grabs some rags.*

YEW: And if you're thinking weird thoughts about that fellow—forget it.

SISSY: Yewina!

YEW: You just met him and he'll be on his way as soon's the tow truck gets here, or I fix his rig, or Dan comes on Monday, or whatever comes first. So don't go acting weird, fergawdsakes. People already think you're half-cracked.

SISSY: Who? Who thinks I'm half-cracked?

YEW: Ah . . . Jerry Jones.

SISSY: Gerald Jerry?

YEW: The other one.

SISSY: Jerry Jerome?

YEW: Jerry Gerard.

SISSY: Oh I don't care about him. Two out of three Jerrys think I'm ...

SISSY makes the thumbs up sign.

A-1!

YEW: That's not the point. The point is, that nice fellah is going to leave and until he does, you're going to behave. You wanted company, now we got some so, act normal for once. All right?

SISSY: All right.

YEW: Promise?

SISSY: ... Promise.

YEW: Good.

SISSY: But what is it like? I mean the sex. / What's it like?

YEW: / Aaaargh!! What did I just say?

SISSY: But it's normal right? Does your skin feel what their skin feels, hands touchin' hands, reaching out—

YEW: Sure, whatever.

SISSY: Was it like your body melts where his fingers touch—

YEW: Yeah, I s'pose.

SISSY: —and the way you feel down there ...

YEW: Oh boy.

SISSY: ... all warm ripples and—

YEW: Yeah, yeah whatever.

SISSY: Well, what was it like?

YEW: Fertheluvvacripes. It's like . . .

SISSY: Well?

YEW: I'd rather have a good shit.

SISSY: No! Shut up.

YEW: True.

SISSY: No! You're just being mean.

YEW: I am not having this conversation with you now. I got a car to fix.

SISSY: Why does everybody in the world do it?

YEW: C'mon now, don't go feeling sorry for yourself.

SISSY: All the time everybody but me.

YEW: Well, maybe they like it.

SISSY: Why? What's is like?

YEW: It's like whatever, it's like—parsnips! Do you like parsnips?

SISSY: No.

YEW: Too bad, some people do.

> *YEW goes to leave, SISSY stops her.*

SISSY: —Yewina?

YEW: What?

SISSY: Do you think . . . maybe my real mother isn't in Hollywood. Am I like a half-thing? Like Mom did have me but with someone like Richie MacCritchie or Daddy got someone pregnant like Phyllis Gillis or Innis McInnis and nobody wanted me and that's why I—

YEW: —Look! You found were in a nest . . . maybe you came from an egg.

SISSY: Pshaw right! Like I don't know that's unpossible.

YEW: Why not?

SISSY: Ah, I'm a mamminal.

YEW: Mammal.

SISSY: Yes. We're all mamminals.

YEW: Mam—ach. Platypuses come from eggs.

SISSY: Wha'? Are they mamminals?

YEW: Mammals.

SISSY: Are they?

YEW: I don't know, does it matter? They're warm and furry and weird just like you and they come from an egg in Australia.

SISSY: I could be from Australia?

YEW: Yeah, think about that for a while. Now, I got an engine to look at.

YEW exits. SISSY thinks.

SISSY: Aaaaau-sssstraaal-ia . . .

SCOTT returns.

SCOTT: I just got their answering machine, looks like they're closed for the weekend.

SISSY: *(happy)* Eeee!

(covering) Oh that's too bad. Yewina's looking at it right now though and you can stay here, you can stay by the stove, it's nice.

SCOTT: I feel terrible putting you folks out.

SISSY: You ever seen a platypus?

SCOTT: Ah, no.

SISSY: Well, guess we're not related!

SCOTT's puzzled but SISSY carries on.

Cookie?

SCOTT: Sure, thanks. Um well, I should probably go see—

SISSY: Why'd you come up here, all the way from the desert?

SCOTT: I didn't come straight here. I was in Toronto for a while.

SISSY: Collecting folkloreses?

SCOTT: Oh no, no, I was sort of the drummer in my girlfriend's post-punk art-school band, the Fur-Lined Teacups.

SISSY chuckles.

SISSY: . . . Teacups. But why'd you come here?

SCOTT: The band voted me out—said I looked too bourgeois.

SISSY: So you came here?

SCOTT: I was in PEI for a while, working on a women's collective emu farm with my fiancée at the time.

SISSY: PEI!

SCOTT: Yup, beautiful. Small though. Whoohee everybody knows everybody—

SISSY: So then you came here?

SCOTT: Yeah, with another woman from the farm. She saved me from a rogue emu attack and—well, long story short, we sort of had to leave the island. Anyway, she started a summer theatre festival on the mainland. I helped out—

SISSY: Acting?

SCOTT: Pumping the septic. You know . . .

SISSY: *(pretending to know)* Theatre.

SCOTT: Yeah, but that ended.

SISSY: The theatre?

SCOTT: That too. But one of the actresses I uh, sort of met, was in the Folklore Studies program and now here I am, only a thesis away from getting a masters in Ethnology and Folklore.

SISSY: You've done so many difdrent things. That's amazing.

SCOTT: Is it? My folks say I can't stick to anything, but I think I'm on track now. It's been a long haul but I finally feel like I'm, like I'm a—

SISSY: Whacking your balls on the freeway!?

SCOTT: What? Oh golf! Fairway. But yeah, you could say that.

YEW enters.

YEW: Well, it might be a transmission leak. I put a piece of cardboard down, we'll see in the morning. Sorry you won't get to meet Doc MacMaster. He's a nice old coot.

SCOTT: Yes, I was looking forward to recording him, telling the legend of the deep-channel mermaid.

SISSY: Legend?   **YEW:** Mermaid?

SCOTT: His letter mentioned a local legend of a fisherman who married a mermaid.

SISSY & YEW: Francis Bouchie?

SCOTT: That was the name, do you know it?

SISSY: It's not a legend. I told Doc MacMaster about it, why would he say it was a legend?

YEW: Having little strokes, probably.

SISSY: Oh right. Well. It happened, before our time but Francis Bouchie caught a mermaid in the channel. She musta been chasing the mackerel—he was hauling traps, tugging and hauling and he thought, "What's that coming outta the water?" It looked like beautiful, wild hair and he thought it was a drowning girl, but it was a mermaid with long, long beautiful red seaweed hair and golden eyes, all gold, and skin as blue as October water and her bottom end was like a fish but covered in the softest seal fur—right, Yewina?

YEW: That's what they say.

SISSY: Yup and I guess she was right nice to talk to, so he brought her home. It was dark though when he'd carried her into the house and in the night she started to get older and meaner, until by morning she was just a mean, ugly old woman and she ate his cat. So, he went to throw her back into the sea and whoosh, she turned into the beautiful girl again and he got all mooshy and hauled her out again and again she turned into the hag. He spent the whole winter hauling her out and throwing her back until one day he went out for her and she was gone. And so was every cat from Cape Jack to Jimtown.

SCOTT: Why did she eat cats?

SISSY: I don't know. But she was a mermaid so there's probably a scien-terrific explanation.

SCOTT: You told this to Dr. MacMaster.

SISSY: Sure when I had to go to him for my ner—   *YEW coughs.*

SISSY: —eerrrv-accimations. My nervaccimations. Anyway he was always um, nice to talk to and he's not from here so he loved for me to be telling him who everybody was and what all. It's not a legend. Francis Bouchie lived just over the rise acrost from where the wharf was.

SCOTT: Wow. Listen, could I record you?

SISSY: Sure!

SCOTT: I'll just get my notebook and stuff from the car . . . .

He leaves.

YEW: Behave.

SISSY: Oh my god, he played in a band and he's been everywhere, Yewina, even PEI, and his grandfather was a Comanche—

YEW: Comanche? Thought he said Cherokee.

SISSY: And his grandfather rode a pony! A palomino, a palomino Comanche pony!

YEW: Palomino? Oh my god, look—don't go building things up. Remember what happened with Tommy.

SISSY: That was difdrent. And I'm not building thi—

YEW: It's getting dark, go put the chickens to bed. Go.

SISSY complies.

Motheragod, s'gonna a long weekend.

Scene Three

The next morning SCOTT *is sleeping serenely on the kitchen cot.* SISSY *is watching him close-up, intently. She's holding an egg. In his dream he feels her presence. John Arthur crows.* SCOTT's *eyelids flutter open—her face is in his.*

SCOTT: Ahh . . . ?

SISSY: For you. Sheila. She laid this for you. How do you like it?

SCOTT: Oh, scrambled? Thanks and thank Sheila but—I kinda don't start with breakfast for a while—any chance of a coffee?

SCOTT yawns and rubs his eyes.

SISSY: Oh, sure yup, yup coffee. Yewina likes coffee too! I got the water on all ready.

SISSY puts the egg in her lap and presents him with an old shoe stuffed with tissue.

And this . . . this is my caul.

She unwraps a bit of the tissue to show him her caul.

SCOTT: Holy cow. Euw. Wow, I have never seen a real, a real dried . . . amniotic membrane.

SISSY: It's my caul. It will protect you.

SCOTT: Thanks . . . I'm feeling pretty safe. Actually it's a little early in the day for . . . for ah, cauls too. Can we put that aside to look at later?

SISSY: Sure! You take milk? We got canned.

Somewhere in the following scene, SISSY takes the shoe and caul back to the counter to make coffee.

SCOTT: Black's fine.

SISSY: You want some sugar? Ha, ahahaha sugar—like me! Whoah—I'm sweet enough to put me in yer cup! Hahaha! That's me, they called me Sugar 'cause I was a sugar ti—

SCOTT: Yup.

SISSY: Just . . . joking. I wouldn't fit in your cup.

SCOTT: Ah, haha. Yeah, no. No sugar thanks though, Sugar—I mean Sissy.

SCOTT gets his pants on under the quilt and tries to think of conversation.

I passed a ruined mansion, in some old pasture, with turrets—any ghosts or legends there?

SISSY stands with her back to SCOTT, making coffee. Perhaps even off stage.

SISSY: That's Brophy Castle.

SCOTT: Brophy Castle?

SISSY: Alphonse Brophy built it with bags of money he made on rum-rumming.

SCOTT: So . . . that'd be in the twenties, thirties?

SISSY: He had one daughter Marcella and all the fellahs were after her or—as Daddy used to say, "Are they after her or are they after the old man's money?" Anyhow, her best friend was Penny Pelley.

YEW enters.

YEW: The Pelleys from the dump?

(then, to SCOTT) How'd you sleep?

SCOTT: Fine thanks.

SISSY: Oh my god, Marcella had pale, pale skin like moonlight and long, long snow-white hair and eyelashes like white frost flowers.

YEW: Penny was some funny looking though.

SISSY: People said Penny was as homely as Marcella was beautiful but, holy cow, she was crazy for Marcella. And people didn't know this but they got married.

YEW: Well... **SISSY:** Yeah! When we were kids, by Kenny MacNeil, tsk.

YEW: Weird little Kenny MacNeil, tsk, when he was maybe eight years old, was always practising to be a priest.

SCOTT: What do you mean?

SCOTT accepts a coffee from SISSY.

Thanks.

YEW: He'd wear his mother's nightgown and pretend to say mass in the woodshed.

SISSY: —and he did the communion with his mom's silver tea service.

YEW: Foolishness.

SISSY: He made all us kids play along. Even Janice Murray and she was a Protestant. Anyhow, Marcella and Penny were older than us, teenagers, and they got him to marry them. I was the flower girl. Yewina was the best man. He done a real good job. He said everything the real priest would say. And remember, Yewina? They had rings out of rabbit snare wire—'member?

YEW: Ah yeah, I made the rings.

SISSY: Oh yeah. We had everything, even a cake that Penny brang from the dump. So I always figured that they were married.

YEW: Well, by weird little Kenny, tsk, who also baptized Pusscat—

SISSY: Aww, Pusscat.

YEW: —and performed an exorcism on the Murray's dog.

SISSY: Aww Scampy. He was some hyper but after the exor-chisum he calmed right down.

YEW: Uhuh.

SISSY: Anyway Marcella—remember, 'Weena?— When the berry picker's kid got lost? This little boy got lost beyond the mountain—

SCOTT: Berry pickers?

YEW: People used to travel down to pick blueberries. They'd camp on the Brophy property. Well the little boy wandered off beyond the fields, behind the lake into in the deep old, old, old woods—the forgotten forest that's never been cut: shaggy old hemlocks and sugar maples so big your arms can only reach halfway round, ferns and moss deep as a feather bed. People call those woods "The Dream"— Everybody was going nuts searching, it was pretty scary. He was only a little fellah. Marcella wanted to help look—

SISSY: —but her eyesight wasn't too good, hey? So. She took off her shoes and she just felt with her feet all the little trails that are there that you don't really see, the mouse trails, the rabbit runs, the deer paths and holy gee, she followed until she found the little boy way back of beyond, deep in the Dream, crying by the lake. Didn't she, Yewina?

YEW: That's what she said.

SISSY: And she said they could hear the coggar breathing and growling and prowling and they didn't know what to do, but the little fella hopped in her lap and she took her long white hair and shook it around them and made like a tent for them and they sang songs together . . . and the coggar? He circled all night, but he never harmed them and then at dawn he disappeared.

YEW: S'no coggars.

SISSY: Anyhow everybody was so happy they had a big party. There were lots of parties there and Marcella and Penny lived in that big house and they were happy although . . .

YEW: After old man Brophy finally died—

SISSY illustrates cause of death with the universal sign for drinking.

—they discovered he had lost all his money playing the ponies.

SISSY: And—

SISSY repeats the universal sign for drinking.

YEW: Anyhow Marcella and Penny were all right even though the house was falling down around their ears.

SISSY: And then this one time—only the one time, remember, 'Weena— they invited everybody on the road in for a big ceilidh! Penny played the fiddle, hey?

YEW: She was some good. Made up her own tunes and everything.

SISSY: Yup, and there was every kind of food and! They opened the last case of Alphonse's real French champlain.

SCOTT: Wow.

YEW: Yup.

SISSY: Oh, it was the best party you ever saw. And the next day after everybody left, Marcella and Penny drug their big bed into the kitchen, poured themselves the last of that real French champlain, hopped in bed and turned on the gas.

YEW: Turns out nobody knew it but Penny had the cancer pretty bad so— yeah, they ah, whew, they decided to go out together.

YEW's a little verklempt.

SISSY: Marcella woulda been all alone. So they done the gas.

YEW: Was Uncle Dunc found them the next morning . . .

SISSY: Yeah.

YEW: He went over, looking for a drink of rum for his hangover . . .

SISSY: . . . and there they were in the bed . . . Holding each other in their beautiful silk niggala, naygala—

YEW: Negligees.

SISSY: Negligents. Beautiful silk negligents. Arms around each other. Dead. And the rigor morons had set in.

YEW: Mortis.

SISSY: Father MacFeeney said they had to be buried separate and told Isaac the undertaker, "Break them, break their limbs!"

SCOTT: That's barbaric!

YEW: Who's going say no to a priest.

SISSY: Isaac snapped their arms and legs with a crowbar and maul.

SCOTT: Yegods, that's horrific.

SISSY: Yup. I think it was after that, Isaac's face twitches started.

YEW: Yeah.

SISSY: Yeah. But you know what? We snuck in at night—didn't we, Yewina? And we saw them, in their separate coffins in separate rooms, and! They had the rabbit snare rings on! On their poor, broken fingers—'member, 'Weena?

YEW: Jeezis, I wish I could forget it.

SISSY: They were in separate coffins but had their rings. Because they were married.

YEW: Well, married by weird little Kenny, tsk, in the woodshed.

SISSY: Poor little Kenny, tsk, but he did go on to the cinnamon-ary.

YEW: Seminary.

SISSY: He was ordained.

YEW: Ordained. I don't think it's retroactive with the priest thing.

SISSY: Ah, I think it is.

YEW: Poor Kenny, tsk.

SISSY: Yeah, tsk, he went to Uganda with the Scarboro Missions and died . . . from a brain worm? I think it was a brain worm. / Was it a brain worm?

YEW: Brain worm? Yeah it was a brain worm.

SISSY: Brain worm.

YEW: Brain worm?

SISSY: Brain worm.

SCOTT: Brain worm?

SISSY: Brain worm.   **YEW:** Brain worm. Yup.

SISSY: Yup, died of a brain worm, poor little Kenny / tsk.

YEW: / Tsk.

SCOTT: Wow, that's a tragic tale.

YEW: Least they went out with a party.

SISSY: And in silk negligents!

YEW sighs.

SCOTT: Well, that's a very interesting story.

SISSY: Is that a good story for your collecting.

SCOTT: Ah, that's not really my area.

YEW: Alrighty, let me look at your rig again. Could be the transmission fluid is leaking.

> *YEW keeps talking off stage. Dialogue can be the actor's choice. It's a Doppler-esque effect. E.g., "If it's a slow leak I got a bottle of sealer somewhere—but if it's a goddamn computer chip I'd say we're hooped, good engine though, cast iron, good model, before Volvo sold her out, but the frikkin' dealership prices, oh my jeeeezis . . ." Use as much or as little as need be.*

SCOTT: *(accepting coffee)* Thanks, Sissy, and thank you for the mermaid story, do you know anyone in town who would know that or any other stories like it?

SISSY: I guess you could ask the Jerrys, but Gerard's a bullshitter and Jerome is clueless, and Gerald is— Nah, forget the Jerrys. And if Mom and Daddy were here they could tell you . . . but they um . . .

SCOTT: They're gone are they? I'm sorry, when did they pass?

SISSY: Oh jeez, I think they're still kicking. They abrandoned us.

SCOTT: Abandoned?— I'm sorry to hear that.

SISSY: Yeah, they left us, never to return . . . Don't tell Yewina I told you, she gets right sad 'cause she's touchy about being abrandoned. I guess since I was kinda abrandoned from the get-go, it's not so hard on me. Oh—you're not going to write that down are you?

SCOTT: No, no that's not the kind of story I'm collecting.

SISSY: Why not collect Marcella and Penny's story? That's a good story.

SCOTT: It sure is from a vernacular point of view, you know—gossip.

SISSY: Oh.

SCOTT: But it's not the area of my research. I'm gathering older accounts, specifically those with supernatural or mythic content—legends. So thank you for the mermaid story, at least it's something to take back. But with Dr. MacMaster no longer in a coherent state, it looks like I've missed the real chance. Dead end again. So much for my overdue, underwritten thesis. Anyway . . . I should see if I can help your sister with the car and then I'll be on my way and outta your hair.

SISSY: The Grinder!

SCOTT: Sorry.

SISSY: The Grinder. Ever hear of him?

SCOTT: No . . .

SISSY: S'gotta be probably the oldest, most legend-est story in these parts—the Grinder, yeah. Sometimes I think the coggar must be like his fifty-seven-hundreds-something great grandson.

SCOTT: Who—what is the Grinder?

SISSY: This goes back hey, like before the pioneers, maybe from the French time. Come to think, I'm pretty sure they heard it right from the Mi'kmaq.

SCOTT: Really?

SISSY: Yup the Grinder was a terrible, horrible thing that lived at the bottom of the lake back of the mountain. And the Grinder just hated the people. Back in them days, this one chief, he built a big, long house for all his warriors, and they'd have a big fire—

SCOTT: Oh yeah?

SISSY: —in the middle of the house and—

SCOTT, half listening, indicates the coffee pot.

SCOTT: Mind if I hot it up—?

SISSY: Sure, let me do it—

SISSY jumps up to help him pour and then follows him back to the couch, where he gets comfortable while she talks.

Yeah, anyhow, the warriors'd sit 'round the big fire and they'd get smoking and feasting all night until the fire died to ashes and they'd pass out and that just rotted the old Grinder to hear all the fun and carousing, rotted him out with jealousy and rage so he snuck in at night when they were all sleeping and grabbed one of the fellows by the heel and tore into him, drinking his blood—!

SCOTT: Like a vampire?

SISSY: Worse! And the next morning everybody woke up to see the bones and they were like, "Oh my frig. This can't be real!" So that night, they partied again until they passed out and holy jeely, again the Grinder picked another poor fella, tore his guts out and on it went like this, night after night. Nobody could do nothing and they all were going crazy until, across the bay there, the biggest bruiser in Harbour D'Espoir, Blaise DeWolfe, heard about the Grinder and he hopped in his canoe, came over the bay and told the chief, "Don't you worry. I got this." Then he tucked down for the night with the other fellahs and waited and the others fell asleep and he waited and the fire died down and he waited . . . and then— ahhhrgh! The Grinder picked off the guy next to him! Well, DeWolfe jumped up and grabbed the Grinder by the arm and the fight was on— the Grinder didn't know what the hell from what—and they fought and they fit, and they fit and they fought, until all at once—cracking and ripping the bones—DeWolfe tore the friggin' arm right off the Grinder's shoulder!

SCOTT: Tore his arm off?

SISSY: Yeah! And the howling? I guess it'd turn your hair white! You could hear it all acrost the bay and back! The ol' Grinder was licked. He slunk off back to his lake to die. And the warriors were whooping and hollering and carrying Blaise DeWolfe on their shoulders and all right happy but—but what they didn't know was the Grinder? The Grinder had a mother . . .

SCOTT: Mother?

SISSY: And oh, she was—

SCOTT: Could you stop for a minute, Sissy . . .

(then to himself) Holy shit.

SISSY: There's more to it.

SCOTT: Cool, cool—hold that thought wouldya—I gotta make a call.

> *He is gathering paper, pen, etc., . . . distracted. SISSY thinks he didn't like the story.*

> *YEW enters.*

YEW: I think it got 'er now.

SISSY: It gets better—

SCOTT: Sorry, guys I just need to make a phone call. Just one call, kinda important—

> *SCOTT exits to the henhouse roof.*

> *YEW pours herself a coffee.*

YEW: I think I found the leak, got 'er plugged up and topped up the transmission fluid. So cross your fingers, he should be able to leave now.

SISSY is near tears, moving in agitation.

Hey, Sissy, whoah what's wrong?

SISSY: He's leaving. Everybody leaves.

YEW: He's gotta get back to the university. He's got work to do. He can't be lollygagging here.

SISSY: Am I a weirdo?

YEW: No, you're not a weirdo!

SISSY: Does he think I'm half-cracked?

YEW: Listen, Sissy, you're doing good. Well, pretty good, all right?

SISSY: Thanks, Yewina.

YEW: Yeah, and listen, you know before when you asked me about the, ah, Mike and me and that?

SISSY: Yeah. You said you'd rather have a good shit.

YEW: Okay, about that. I was just being mean—

SISSY: Knew it!

YEW: —it was mean of me, so ah, sorry about that.

SISSY: Why are you so mean?

YEW: The thing of it is, sometimes I don't know how else to be, if I'm feeling nervous.

SISSY: You get nervous?

YEW: Cripes, making me talk about sex for the first time in forty million fricking years?

SISSY: Oh yeah. I guess. So you wouldn't rather have a good shit?

YEW: Hm, well some days I might. Anyhow I just thought I should apologize. So. Yeah.

SISSY: Are you sorry that you and Mike did that, had sex?

YEW: Wha'? Oh no, it was all right. Okay?

SISSY: And he had pretty hair.

YEW: And yeah, he had pretty hair. He did. Whew. My hands in that hair . . . He kissed my skinned knuckles. Stars and meteors that night . . . oh boy.

SISSY: You said sex is like parsnips?

YEW: Okay, it's only like parsnips if that's what you like. It's like whatever you like.

SISSY: Hm. Mashed turnips?

YEW: Sure. You like turnips?

SISSY: The real dark, orangie turnips that the frost got to a little bit? Boiled up with a bit of salt and onion and smashed with cream?

YEW: And with butter slathered all over?

SISSY: And a little bit of brown sugar sprinkled on top! So the sugar is crunchy on your teeth but the turnip is all smooth and creamy and the butter drips down your chin a bit.

YEW: It was like that.

SISSY: I like turnips.

YEW: Well.

SISSY: Wow.

YEW: Anyhow, now you know and now that fella can get back in his Volvo and be on his way—

SCOTT returns.

SCOTT: I just called the university. My thesis advisor is as excited as I am. Sissy, I want to record the Grinder story properly—every detail you can remember, where you heard it, who else may know it. This could be an extremely, extremely important variant of the ancient Anglo-Saxon Beowulf legend! If so, a new world Beowulf legend would indicate pre-colonial contact between Vikings and Indigenous peoples. And if so, this could provide corroboration for etiological theories of a Scandinavian origin, and if so point to a Wulfing urtext! And if so this, this could finally be my goddamn thesis!! Could I impose on your hospitality for another few days?

Intermission.

Act Two

Scene Four

Lights up on SISSY and SCOTT. It is after supper.

SISSY: I heard Mom and Daddy whispering about our work horse Delmar. Aww Delmar, he was so pretty, all black with a silver star right here . . .

SISSY indicates her forehead.

They were talking about sending him off to the knackers for dog food—just 'cause he was old and had the heaves and his eyes had cadillacs! So in the middle of the night I snuck out, opened the gate, jumped on Delmar and it was like he already knew where to go. We galloped up the beach to Tommy Day's. Even though Tommy was a boy and was older he was never mean to me. He had the nicest smile and he'd even smile at me. He was difdrent—the other boys, they tripped me and spit spitballs on my neck. Yeah! And they called me a scag and a weirdo and said my real mother tried to drown me.

SCOTT: That's terrible. Guys can be such jerks.

SISSY: Especially Ricky Gruntz. He told me I smelled like chicken bum and I was so ugly nobody would ever want to "eff" me.

SCOTT: God, that's so mean.

SISSY: Yeah but Tommy was difdrent. When I was little, Tommy showed me how to lie on the beach grass and let my eyes see the world like a giant circle. He gave me this—

She hands SCOTT a piece of bayberry.

Smell. It's sweet isn't it? You can still smell that day. That's why I knew what I had to do when it came time to save Delmar. Delmar and me rode up the beach to Tommy's house and I threw pebbles on his window and when he stuck his head out, there we were, with the moonlight shining on old Delmar's star and on my bare arms and I said, "This horse will carry us away—away to the waters and the wild and into the big, round world—come away with me Tommy." And Tommy reached down his hand and I reached up mine and even though our fingers didn't touch, I felt him and he said, "Give me a minute to grab some clothes." And he smiled. And he ducked back in. And he called the police.

SCOTT: Ah no. Holy cow.

SISSY: Yeah. Why did he do that?

SCOTT: I don't know . . . Scared probably.

SISSY: Scared of what? Scared of me?

SCOTT: Oh no, no. People get scared um . . . scared of what they want.

SISSY: Really? Why though?

SCOTT: I don't know. Wish I did.

SISSY: Are you scared of what you want?

SCOTT: I think . . . I'm scared . . . that I don't know what I want.

SISSY: You don't know?

SCOTT: Well until I found folklore studies, I was always on to new things.

SISSY: Hm. Is that bad?

scott: My dad says, "Another phase? When are you going to get in the game and stay in the game? You're all layup and no follow through!" Sorry, I didn't mean to talk about me. I'm sorry Tommy let you down like that.

sissy: Yup. But they never got Delmar—they never sent him to the knackers! When they hauled me off, I let him go and I yelled, "Run, Delmar, run!!" And boys, did he ever! Like a yearling, he ran up the beach and into the woods and they never found him yet.

YEW enters.

yew: Y'talking about Delmar? He's dead.

sissy: Illegibly. Illegibly dead.

yew: Pft, ol' broke wind, sway back nag. Likely starved or drowned or mauled by a bear.

sissy: At least he never got ground up for dog meat.

yew: Story time done?

scott: Done for the day, Sissy's filled in a lot of details of the Grinder story, and we were just chatting.

yew: So. You got all the details you need.

scott: Pretty much.

yew: That's too bad. Means you'll be on your way.

sissy: There's more stories—there's always more stories.

scott: Yes, we could—

YEW: Yeah, but he needs the myths and legends for his thesis, not Delmar the dead horse stories—

SCOTT: Although I'd like—

YEW: —So I guess we're pretty much done, right.

SCOTT: Ah . . . did you—if I remember correctly, did you earlier mention, fairies?

SISSY: The fairies are all on the other side of the river.

YEW: There's no such—

SISSY: Yes, where it gets marshy, you can see little glowing lights—that's where the fairies dance. The old people used to say that when the fairies really get going with the dancing, they kinda, well, they . . . fart a lot and that's what makes the lights.

YEW: Duh, swamp gas.

SISSY: Duh, fairy farts.

SCOTT: Are there local names for the little people?

YEW: Ethel and Edwin.

SISSY gasps.

Shoot.

SCOTT: Who?

YEW and SISSY exchange a look.

YEW: Okay I guess, you're not from here. You won't tell, will ya?

SCOTT crosses his heart holds his fingers up scout's honour style.

Hm. Okay. See, Doc and Mrs. MacMaster had twins. They were born little you know, little people.

SISSY: That's what they call themselves, little people.

SCOTT: Ah, dwarfs.

SISSY & YEW: Little people!

YEW: Is their preferred term.

SCOTT: Gotcha thanks.

YEW: They're not fairy-tale legends.

SISSY: They're real real. Ethel is Yewina's best friend.

YEW: Yeah.

SISSY: But in grade nine, they stopped coming to school.

YEW: The doc stopped them. He had a little house built for them, everything the right size for them, up by the quarry. Not a neighbour near.

SISSY: But they had the bare n'essential-tees.

YEW: Necessities.

SISSY: Yup. I remember after he moved them out, Mrs. Mac showed up here, smelling like rotten plums, kinda tipsly, you know . . .

She makes a drinking sign.

Anyhow, she paid Yewina to go play with Ethel and Edwin.

YEW: Hey, hey, hey, I never took her money. I was already hopping on my bike and going over every day anyways.

SISSY: Yup, every day up to their little house. You were a good friend.

YEW: Well, Ethel was a lot of fun—holy jeez, she could do voices though. She could take off anybody. "I taught I taw a puddy tat! I did I d—" see I can't do voices, but man Ethel, she was . . . yeah. We'd cook fudge—

SISSY: Mmm . . .

YEW: —and read Nancy Drew books, play records and dance—

SISSY: That's Ethel's record player.

Sissy indicates the old record player.

YEW: —we'd just . . . talk and goof around and . . .

SISSY: Practise kissing.

YEW: Hey!

SISSY: For later when you had to kiss for real.

YEW: Cripes, Sissy. Anyway.

SISSY: Ethel was comical though.

YEW: She could make anyone laugh.

SISSY: But Edwin . . . he was angry.

YEW: Well it wasn't fair. To just aban— To exile them like that.

SISSY: But Mrs. MacMaster, she hired Sister Dorothy—

YEW: —she was the French and phys. ed. teacher at the convent—

SISSY: —she hired her to come out and give them lessons. Aww, Sister Dorothy she had a face like a saucer of milk with big green eyes. She was young and when she laughed, she giggled with her hand over her mouth.

YEW: Alls I remember is being jealous. I woulda loved having my own house built for me, no one telling me what to do. But Edwin'd take off and sleep out in the quarry. He'd come back on the days Sister Dorothy came though, and they'd go down to the brook to do lessons. Come to think, Ethel never did any lessons . . . that was fine by her. Anyhow this went on for a while and then one day I went down as usual and there was the door, flapping open . . . I go in and the whole place was wide open empty— raccoons setting on the little chairs at the little table—but all the clothes, books, gone.

SISSY: Yewina took the record player.

YEW: Yeah. Turns out Mrs. Mac had sold her jewellery, and—look don't repeat this—because the doc can't know where they are, but . . . Mrs. Mac bought them tickets to Paris, France.

SCOTT: Ethel and Edwin?

YEW: And Dorothy.

SCOTT: Sister Dorothy?

YEW: She chucked the "Sister" part. I guess Edwin and Dorothy were . . . you know . . .

SISSY: "Lovers."

YEW roll her eyes.

Which is weird you know because he was a—you know? He was / aaaaaa—

SCOTT: / Dwarf?

SISSY: —lot younger than her.

A puzzled pause before SCOTT and YEW speak almost simultaneously.

YEW: Little / person.

SCOTT: / Little person, yup.

YEW: Anyhoo, they're happy in Paris. They run a gourmet restaurant. I guess the French are just crazy for fudge.

SISSY: Mmm . . .

SISSY: Ethel still sends Yewina cards.

SISSY references a card stuck on the fridge.

YEW: Joyeux Noël.

SCOTT: And Dr. MacMaster?

YEW: Knows nothing. And he never will.

SCOTT: Gotcha.

YEW: When he found out they'd run away, he blew up, went clean clear clipping spinorky, raging at Mrs. Mac, but she wouldn't give in and tell him where they were, so he had her carted off to live in that expensive "hotel"—

SISSY: *(sotto voce)* Mental hopspital. In Monkreal.

YEW: And he hasn't been the same since.

SISSY: People stopped wanting to go to him.

YEW: Corinne Cameron said she went to him for her psoriasis and he grabbed her hands, weeping and asking her to pray for him and telling her to never have kids.

SISSY: He was a bit like that though, even before the twins left. He used to cry when I went for my ner-eervaccinations.

YEW: He'd cry?

SISSY: Yeah, after he did the breast exclam-bination I'd talk and he'd cry.

YEW: Breast examination?

SISSY: Oh my god could ya stop correcting / everything I say!

YEW: / I'm not correcting—what breast exclam—examination? You were s'posed to be going for your nerves.

SISSY: I was. Every other week all winter. But he always started with a quick breast exclamination—and then I'd talk about my nerves. Ah, sorry, Scott, it wasn't for vaccinations. I had the bad nerves after Tommy turned me down. They're great now though!

YEW: Breast exnam, ex— Wha'?

SISSY: Doc MacMaster said, "Early detection is key in the fight against teen breast cancer"—

YEW: —Teen bre—? He gave you breast exclambil, exlamal—!?

SISSY: Exclambination?

YEW: Oh my god, he was feeling up your boobs.

SISSY: 'Weena! He'd get the exclambination out of the way and then I'd talk—and he'd cry. I'd try and distract him and tell him stuff about—like when Mom climbed the tree sleepwalking and got hit by lightning—

YEW: You told him about Mom?

SISSY: Yeah, or like that time she sleepwalked into your room and chopped all your hair off.

YEW: Oh my god.

SISSY: —or how Mom used to sleep-smash all the dishes or—

YEW: You were s'posed to be going to him for your nerves.

SISSY: But there wasn't much to say—nerves are nerves. / I was just trying to tell him stuff to get him to stop that awful crying. What the chickens were up to—you know this, that, and the other thing.

YEW: *(incoherent rage-mumble)* / That gaddaaaaam, old frickin'—bast— jeezly frigger, son of a whooo—teen bre—? I oughta.

> *YEW gets her gun and shells and mutters direly until SISSY's line is done and then.*

I'm just ah, going, I gotta . . . Don't wait—yous just. Keep chatting—I'll be back.

> *Through this YEW is putting shells in the shotgun, only SCOTT sees her though, as SISSY's back is to YEW. YEW leaves fuming. Optional voice trailing off-stage gag. "That slimey fuckin' sonova who-er, I never liked him, with his goddam scraggly goatee, and that fuckin' cravat with the ol' mustard stains—cravat!? Who's he fuckin' kiddin'? He's from frickin' Truro, cravat my arse! Wait'll I get my . . . "*

SCOTT: Is she going be all right?

SISSY: Oh yeah.

SCOTT: But is she going to—should we do something? Should I—

SISSY: What do you like better, parsnips or turnips?

SCOTT: Sorry?

SISSY: Parsnips or turnips?

SCOTT: I'm not a big root vegetable guy but if I had to pick . . . turnips?

SISSY: Knew it.

SCOTT: Does your sister have any anger control issues—?

SISSY: With butter and brown sugar?

SCOTT: I guess I've never tried them like that, but sure.

SISSY: Knew it!

SISSY: So, golphins?

SCOTT: What?

SISSY: You and your family are big golphins?

SCOTT: Gol-phins? Oh, golfers, no—or yes, they are, but I'm not. Anisometropia, strabismus, and nystagmus.

SISSY: Anisometropia, strabismus, and nystagmus.

SCOTT: How—? Wow. Okay. Yeah, it's my eyes. No depth perception and—ow—

SCOTT stumbles against a chair.

So, no golf for me. See, I was knocked out by a golf ball, when I was twelve. Hit me on my lazy-eye patch side. That's when my folks realized I was never going to be a golfer. So Mom enrolled me in folk dancing.

SISSY: What?

SCOTT: There's my brother Dale teeing off with the back-slapping millionaires' club while I'm stuck in a church basement—the only boy in a Norwegian folk dancing troupe. Yeah. Thanks, Mom.

SISSY: Dancing!

SCOTT: Folk dancing. Pretend Norwegians in the Ari-friggin'-zona desert.

SISSY: Eeee—dancing!

SCOTT: —with six big, mean, sweaty girls—none of 'em giving me the time of day. "Oh look, Dale's caddying on the PGA groupie tour." Meanwhile Birgit—big toothy Birgit Gygur—is calling me a "fairy." Just how every guy wants to spend his high school: the last Norwegian virgin in Arizona.

SISSY: Showme!Wouldyashowme?Canyoushowmehow / yadance?!!

SCOTT: / It's really dumb, whoah, whoah, okay, no—I'm really rusty and my knees are—okay. Okay. Okay!

SISSY: / Oh you need music, music music!!!

> *As SISSY gets the little record player going, SCOTT, muttering excuses, starts to clap, finding the beat and half-heartedly dancing the Hallingdans to something that Ethel and YEW would have played—highly recommend "Sweet Caroline" by Neil Diamond at top volume.*

SCOTT: Jeez, I don't know if I remember. It's da-da—

> *Whatever the rhythm is,* SCOTT *gets more into the dance, remembering tricks and enjoying himself even when he screws it up because* SISSY's *joy is contagious. Scraps of dialogue are suggested here, whatever is needed to make the action work. E.g., "like this—now on the chair, take my hand . . ." Again, not a rewrite licence to go nuts!*

You're great, wow, you're a natural.

> *Perhaps* SISSY *takes off her sweater and dances around him and at one point he could kick the sweater out of her hand—classic Hallingdans move. Their playfulness becomes slightly erotic. They stop, look at each other, panting and . . .* SISSY *kisses him . . .*

SISSY: Is this what you want, Scott?

SCOTT: Yes! Yes—what about your sister? What if she comes back?

SISSY: To the henhouse!

> *Passionate kissing out the door and up the ladder to the roof of the henhouse, pieces of clothing dropping as they fumble upwards. "Oohs and ahs" and bits of improv, "Get the ladder . . . " They have disappeared to the roof when* YEW *appears. She sees the mess.*

YEW: What in the hell . . .

> *She/we become aware of vocalizing and thumping coming from the roof of the henhouse.*

—coggar!

> YEW *grabs the gun and heads outside—*BOOM! *Chicken squawking,* SCOTT *screams! Lights out.*

Scene Five

Lights up. SCOTT *is bent over a chair, holding* SISSY*'s hand, while* YEW, *wielding tweezers, picks bloody birdshot out of his butt, dropping the pellets on a tin saucer.*

YEW: . . . All right . . . there!

SCOTT: Arh . . . holy fuuuuu . . .

Some birth-style panting.

SISSY: It won't scar, Scott. Mom sleep-shot Daddy once, and it never left a mark.

YEW: Stop squirming, you're making it worse.

SCOTT: Do all the women in your family like to shoot men?

YEW: *(ignoring the question)* There. Nope wait.

Another one.

There! Wait . . . False alarm. Okay you'll live.

YEW slaps SCOTT*'s painful rump.*

SCOTT: Oww!!

YEW: Now get out of our house and don't make me shoot you again.

SISSY: Yewina! She didn't mean that, Scott. Yewina's very sorry for what she did. Right? Right? Yewina, I think you should apologize.

Pause.

YEW: I am very sorry, Scott, that I shot you in the arse while you were humping my sister.

SISSY: Thank you, Yewina.

SCOTT: Yeah.

YEW: You're welcome.

She picks up the gun and places it in its spot by the door.

SCOTT: Could you not—could you put that thing somewhere else, like out of the house please, like far away? Thank you.

YEW glares but grabs the gun and takes it off stage, away from the door.

Owwwowow.

He forgets himself and collapses in a chair, setting off his tender arse.

Ah! Owww...

SISSY: Here—perch on your good side.

She puts her sweater or pillows down. He gingerly sets himself down, leaning to one side.

SCOTT: *(as YEW returns)* Is this what you did to Dr. MacMaster?

YEW: I went through the woods, right to his house and I practically ripped the hinges off the door kicking it open and there he was all startled. I stuck the gun between his eyes and said, "You touched my sister and now I'm going to blow your head off." And he started with the crying and shaking and he was calling me Edwin. "Oh Edwin, my boy! Edwin, don't hurt me!" And the crying coming out of him was that horrible crying, all gulpy and snotty—

SISSY: Yeah, I know.

YEW: —and then he was grabbing at my hands and blubbering . . . and I don't know, all of a sudden it didn't feel right. Shooting him woulda been too much of a mercy. He looked up at me and I said, "Well I know what you are even if you don't." And just like that, I saw at the bottom of his runny, gummy pink eyes, this little flash—like a rat tail disappearing—and I thought, "By god, he understands." So I said, "Yeah, you know, and you know I know, and now you can fricking well live with yourself you sad, sick bastard."

SISSY: Yeah, that was probably enough.

YEW: And then I walloped him right in the old-man nutsack and left.

SISSY: Or maybe not. Thanks, Yewina. I think.

YEW: No problem. Listen, Sissy, shouldn't you be putting them hens to bed?

SISSY: Oh yeah. I have to tell Sheila about us, Scott.

SISSY kisses him and runs out.

SCOTT: I've been thinking—

YEW: No, no you haven't. You gotta go right now, all right.

SCOTT: Excuse me? I care for your sister and not just because of my thesis. I mean I'll be forever grateful for the Beowulf story but I also really care for Sissy.

YEW: Good for you, but you're still gonna take your chivalrous, buckshotted arse outta here.

SCOTT: Sissy can make up her own mind—

YEW: Oh she will. She always does but she doesn't need you anymore. She's got the gist of it now, thank you very much—the story of the great lover from Arizona! And she'll be telling that to the chickens from now till Judgment Day.

SCOTT: Don't mock us. This is a real thing.

YEW: You betcha, yeah real thing, you're more than real. You'll make a good story all right. Only sometimes, instead of rolling in here in a busted Volvo, you'll ride up on a white horse.

SCOTT: What?

Scene Six / Intercut

Split scene. We are in simultaneous places. YEW and SCOTT arguing in the kitchen while we also see SISSY talking with Sheila outside. Lights might shift our attention between spaces, Sheila may cluck and comment where it feels right to.

SISSY: With a gold star right here . . .

SISSY repeats the motion of Delmar's star.

And I lay down and we kissed, and his mouth tasted like August meadow. After that long kiss, I near lost my breath! Yes. He said I was a flower of the mountain. So, yes we are flowers . . .

YEW: But sometimes it'll be just the facts—

SISSY: It was shaped like . . .

She's drawing the shape of a penis in the air for Sheila.

And felt, hm not velvety really but kinda . . . mushroomy?

YEW: Other times she'll treasure every detail—whether they happened or not.

SISSY: And he kissed me with the kisses of his mouth . . . His wings were the color of early morning!

YEW: The same only different every time.

SISSY: Wings the color of winter night!

Sheila cluckclucks.

Yes, I know John Arthur has wings too—but believe me, it's very different with Scott—it's beautiful . . . he circled my breast with a soft feather and then holding me, we flew up with just one beat of his wings, we whooshed up and then he wrapped me in his wings and we drifted down again.

YEW: You'll be better in her stories than you could ever be in life. And you should be happy with that.

SCOTT: Your sister should get a choice.

YEW: Choice? What the use of that?

SCOTT: I can show her the world. I can take her to Halifax.

YEW: You really don't know what you've got here.

SCOTT: You're unbelievable.

YEW: And you're overstaying your welcome, now get out or I will knock you down.

SCOTT: No you won't.

YEW: Oh yeah, why won't I.

SCOTT: Because Sissy loves me.

SISSY: I lay there wrapped in wings. He said I was beautiful . . . his breath in my hair, tickling, his tongue—

Sheila protests.

Oh, you're just jealous, Sheila. People-sex is difdrent—difdrent from ol' John Arthur with his a-pesterin' and a-peckerin'. The air smelled like frost but where we touched was warm and we laughed and laughed . . . and then there was a bang *(makes a gunshot sound)* like thundrel and he yelled and suddenly his tears were in my mouth.

SISSY sighs.

Lights down on Sheila and SISSY. Perhaps they wander off.

YEW: One way or the other, you're going.

SCOTT: If I go, I will ask Sissy to come with me. What do you think she'll say?

YEW: You think she'll fit in with your swanky friends at the university?

SCOTT: She's the real thing and I work with people who have great reverence for authenticity—the kind Sissy has.

YEW: You'll put her on display?

SCOTT: You know what I mean. Not only the Beowulf story but all her stories, we can record them, preserve them perhaps disseminate—disseminate means—

YEW: I know what disseminate means you fu— Listen, right now, her stories, are hers. And anyways, they're only about three-legged dogs and old drunks and old wives' charms to keep the milk fresh. What does that mean to a bunch of strangers. Is there anyone at the university who knows our crowd? No. They want to file us away as "quaint"—

SCOTT: They want to understand and to document and / to—

YEW: / To laugh at us. 'Cause every time she'll tell her stories, she'll tell them wrong because the real authentic version will be sitting in your dead library with a million other stories from people who don't matter to us any more than we matter to them. Is that what you want to do to her? Because the best thing about her stories now—true or not—the best thing is they're never the same twice.

SCOTT: I know she invents spontaneously and embellishes but I can help her clarify and bring her back to the original versions.

YEW: Oh my frig, you really don't have the brains god gave a smelt. Okay. Okay.

> *She picks out a book,* The Norton Anthology, *and tosses it to him.*

Think fast.

> *SCOTT catches the book, startled.*

SCOTT: *The Norton Anthology of / Eng—*

YEW: *English Literature,* yeah.

SCOTT: Where'd—

YEW: —I did a year of college. I started a degree in Home Economics.

SCOTT: You in an apron?

YEW: Don't be smart. Modern Home Economics offers a range of rewarding career options in a challenging world. Now, page seventy-three.

SCOTT: What does this have to do with—?

YEW: Page seventy-three!

SCOTT: All right . . .

> *He turns to page seventy-three and stares at it for a long beat. Closes the book.*

Right.

YEW: So.

SCOTT: So. So, you have a *Norton* in your house, okay, so I did not expect that but so what?

YEW: Page seventy-three?

SCOTT: Yeah.

YEW: Yeah?

SCOTT: Yeah. *Beowulf.* So what? Do you really think that I believe that Sissy Mary, that Sissy reads *The Norton Anthology of English Literature*?

> *SISSY enters.*

SISSY: Sheila's really happy for me, although I don't know if she gets how difdrent people-love is, boy—

YEW: Hey, Sissy—*Northanger Abbey*—how's that go again?

SISSY: *(recites by rote)* "No one who had ever seen Catherine Morland in her infancy would have supposed her to be born to be a heroine."

SCOTT: What . . . ?

SISSY: "Her situation in life, the character of her father and mother, her own person and disposition, were all equally against her."

SCOTT: What are you doing?

SISSY: We only have six books, so I kinda have them all mesmerized.

YEW: Memorized—hey, *Riders of the Purple Sage*.

SISSY: "A sharp clip-crop of iron-shod hoofs deadened and died away, and clouds of yellow dust drifted from under the cottonwoods / out over the sage."

SCOTT: / How does she do that? Wha—?

SISSY carries on under SCOTT and YEW's dialogue as needed.

SISSY: / "Jane Withersteen gazed down the wide purple slope with dreamy and troubled eyes. A rider had just left her, and it was his message that held her thoughtful and almost sad, awaiting the churchmen who were coming to resent and attack her right to befriend a Gentile . . . "

YEW: / Yeah. Impressive, isn't it?

SCOTT: That doesn't necessarily prove anything—

YEW: Bullshit. I'm telling you, buddy, she's been reading that thing all winter every winter, for years.

SCOTT: —if I can find corroborating accounts or . . . / or . . . if I can . . .

YEW: / Sissy! Sissy, hey—*Nancy Drew: The Secret of the Old Clock*!

SISSY: Ethel's favourite! "Nancy Drew, an attractive girl of / eighteen—"

SCOTT: / This can't be happening.

SISSY: / "—was driving home in her new dark blue convertible. She had just delivered some legal papers for / her fa—"

SCOTT: / *Beowulf.*

SISSY: *Beowulf*! "Hark! We shieldlings in days of yore, of glory—"

(Alternative Anglo-Saxon choice: "Hwæt We Gardena in geardagum"—Hey, we spear Danes in old days.")

SISSY realizes too late.

Oh . . . um.

SCOTT: Sissy, did you make up the Grinder story after you read *Beowulf?*

SISSY: Ah . . . that's a really good question.

SCOTT: Oh my god. What the hell?! Do you realize I have an entire department in a frenzy because of my discovery of a New World variant of the Beowulf legend. A discovery with enormous ramifications for folkloric and Indigenous studies, ethnology, history, and—you name it—everything.

SISSY: It's a good story, isn't it? Maybe I read it. Maybe somebody told me.

SCOTT: Sissy! You said it came from "before the pioneers, from the French time who heard it from the Mi'kmaq."

SISSY: Maybe I shouldn't have told it. Maybe it's not my story to tell? Is that the bad part . . .

SCOTT: Yes!

SISSY: I'm sorry. Will it really, really matter?

SCOTT: Will it matter? Oh god, I have to phone my thesis adviser.

SISSY: I'm sorry.

SCOTT: I have to stop her before she contacts any more people—

He gets his phone out and runs out to the henhouse, SISSY turns to YEW.

SISSY: Did you just trick me? You did.

YEW: It's better than letting that fool carry on. Come on, Sissy, sooner or later your story woulda come to light and everything woulda hit the fan.

SISSY: Maybe not. You don't want me to have any fun. Why? Just 'cause you lost Mike Dunagan to Donna Dumphy? That's not my fault.

YEW: I want you to have fun—but you have to stay safe—remember what happ—?

SISSY: Don't start on me about Tommy. At least I took a chance. He was scared but I wasn't. You don't want me to have anything that everybody else has—

YEW: Like what? You got everything here—what more do you want?

SISSY: Well, a libary card would be nice! Why don't we have a libary card?

YEW: I don't / know.

SISSY: / We might not be in this mess right now, if we'd / had a libary card!

YEW: / Okay, okay we'll get / one.

SISSY: / Libaries are important!

YEW: Yes / I know they are.

SISSY: They offer a range of community / services.

YEW: I said okay!

> *Suddenly, off stage there is an unearthly howling mixed with the shrieks of murthered chickens and crashing noises.*

SISSY: The coggar!!!

> *SISSY runs out towards the chaos. Perhaps SCOTT falls off the henhouse roof, past the kitchen window. The howling is hair-raising, otherworldly, not the literal sound of a cougar.*

No, Sissy, noooo! My gun, my gun, my gee-dee gun!

> *YEW runs off stage in the opposite direction to the chaos. The sounds crescendo and stop. Silence and then SCOTT limps in.*

SCOTT: I saw it—I saw it—I looked in its eyes as it leaped over me.

> *YEW enters with the gun but she is too late.*

YEW: / Sissy! Where's Sissy?

SCOTT: Its eyes went right through me . . .

> *SISSY appears in the doorway holding the bloody corpses of Sheila and John Arthur.*

YEW: Oh no . . .

SISSY: . . . Oh, Sheila, my Sheila. Sheila, daughter of Bella Beag, daughter of Hoppy of Crook Leg of Big Bella Mor of Doodle Annie daughter of Sally Two of Sally One, daughter of Speckle Neck of Cynthia of Black Hen Four of Black Hen Three of Black Hen Two beloved daughter of Black Hen the First, the Brooder, the Saviour. Gone, all gone and not a chick remains. No nieces of little One Eye, pecked before her time. Oh, Eleanor carried off by a fox, your sisters are gone. All gone. No chick, nor child now. All for nothing. Gone and lost. And you poor John Arthur, brave John Arthur, bless you! You died for your girls, and for naught. None of your line now survive. None to remember, none to tell. Gone, all gone. The end of stories . . .

SCOTT moves to comfort her.

SCOTT: Sissy, I'm so sorry. It's my fault the door was open. I took the ladder away to get on the roof. I'm so sorry, please . . .

YEW also moves to comfort her. SISSY turns to her.

SISSY: The coggar . . . is not 'stinct.

SCOTT: Where is he?

SISSY: He's gone and so are all my pretty chickens . . . in one fell swoop, the girls of the henhouse, and Sheila too with John Arthur atop of her, his wings spread, he died shielding her, at the foot of her apple tree . . .

SCOTT: Ssshh . . . sh . . .

YEW: *(to SCOTT)* You go pile up them chickens. We got to get rid of them before that coggar comes back. I'll track—

SISSY: No one will "pile" them up! I will carry them, the sisters of Sheila, to the top of the hill and I will strew them with flowers there, where the fox and the hawk and the small devouring creatures may return them to the earth. Sheila and John Arthur will be buried beneath her tree and in years to come the apples that ripen there will be a remembrance of their courage and a testicle-ment to their love.

YEW: I'm sorry, Sissy, I'll come with you.

SISSY: No. The coggar is gone and will not be back for a long time. We do not need the gun.

SISSY turns to face SCOTT.

I am sorry I ruined your plans, Scott. But thank you for holding me on top of the henhouse. I felt us fly together.

SCOTT: That really did happen, didn't it?

SISSY: Yes, it did. And thank you for showing me your penis. It was funnier looking than I thought it would be but still, in its way . . . very pretty.

SCOTT: Okay.

SISSY: Goodbye, Scott. I hope you keep finding what you want to want.

SCOTT: Thank you, Sissy. Thank you for the dance. I wish, I wish I could . . .

    SISSY kisses him gravely and lovingly on each cheek.

SISSY: I will go now and lay them out for their final farewell.

    SISSY picks up the dead lovers and leaves.

YEW: Guess that's a "no" on chicken stew.

SCOTT: She's not safe. That thing could come back—

YEW: She said it's gone.

SCOTT: How does she know?

YEW: Frigged if I know how she knows. I only know she knows.

SCOTT: This is too much for me.

YEW: Yup.

SCOTT: I thought I finally, finally had it figured out.

YEW: How long have you been working on your thesis?

SCOTT: God, it must be nine? No, ten . . . yeah almost ten . . .

YEW: Ten years?

SCOTT: Months. Ten months. I'm stuck. All I manage to do is come up with new titles. I can't seem to get any farther.

YEW: What were you going to call this one?

SCOTT: "Proto-vestiges and Ur-traces of Translocated Folklore in an Obsolete Culture." Proto meaning primitive, ur meaning first, / trans—"

YEW: / and primitive meaning first and vestiges / meaning traces—

SCOTT: / Yeah, okay, whatever.

YEW: So you coulda called it "First traces" or / "Primitive vestiges"?

SCOTT: / Let's drop it, thank you—

YEW: And what's with this obsolete / thing, whyn'tya—?!

SCOTT: —Okay! It's never going to get written, okay? OKAY! Ah, who am I kidding it's just another "phase." Proto-vestiges, you're right, blah blah so what. I don't really care about getting a master's degree. Yeah, I don't care!! Phew.

YEW: Feel better?

SCOTT: Yes. And no. Where do I go now? God, I can't even collect stories.

YEW: Oh, I think you're leaving with a pretty good story.

SCOTT: Wha'? Oh yeah. Yeah, guess I am.

YEW: You want to get some driving in before the sun sets, you should hit the road.

SCOTT: What time is it?

YEW: 7:39.

SCOTT: *(nods and then realizes)* Comanche . . . !

YEW: What?

SCOTT: I knew it wasn't Cherokee. My grandfather, he was seven thirty-ninths Comanche.

YEW: Comanche. Of course he was.

> *YEW looks to where SISSY exited.*

SCOTT: Or is it nine thirty-sevenths? Anyway . . . I only met him a couple of times, when I was little.

> *He picks up his kit bag, recorder, looks around to ascertain that that is everything.*

. . . Thanks, for fixing the palomino, this will probably be her last hurrah . . .

YEW: Palomino?

SCOTT: Oh yeah, I guess that's what my grandfather used to call it, his "palomino pony" probably because of that butterscotch-y colour.

YEW: Palomino Comanche pony . . .

SCOTT: Yeah, when my grandfather started, y'know declining, and couldn't drive anymore, my mother got him put into a home—a good one—up in Oklahoma. He told Mom to give the car to me.

YEW: Right.

SCOTT: Well . . . I guess . . .

YEW: Happy trails.

SCOTT: Fersure, you too . . . and thank you for—

YEW: Go see your grandfather.

SCOTT: Pardon?

YEW: Go see him.

SCOTT: But he's pretty out of it and—

YEW: Take the palomino. Go see him.

SCOTT: I wouldn't want to upset—

YEW: G'wan, s'git outta here.

SCOTT: But ah—

YEW: You get your fickle, freckled, shot-speckled arse into that gee dee palomino car and go see your grandfather—NOW!

SCOTT hightails it out the door. He briefly pokes his head back—

SCOTT: Ca—?

YEW: GET!!

He skitters away to his next adventure. We hear the palomino sputter and leave as YEW gets the tool box. Out of it she takes out a crumpled letter. SISSY comes in.

SISSY: Yewina.

YEW: Sissy. There's something I probably should have told you a long time ago . . .

SISSY: What penises look like?

YEW: No, jeezis would you dropit with the—look. This.

> *YEW holds up a letter.*

This is a letter from Daddy.

SISSY: Where did you get—

YEW: I found it on my bed that day after they aban—aban—

> *It chokes her up to say "abandoned."*

—after they left us.

SISSY: On your bed?

YEW: I didn't want you to feel bad but now I think you should hear what he said . . .

"By the time you read this we will be gone. You know how your mother has always dreamed of seeing Saskatchewan, where I am hoping there will be more room for her sleepwalking hobby. If not, we will keep on and go out to Alberta, weather's good there in the fall. I got some friends that I can go to working for. The good times are all gone and it's time for moving on. What I'm trying to say is I don't expect I will ever see you again. Well, your mother's in the car, honking the horn but there is something you need to know—"

. . . And see there's more writing but I can't make it out, looks like he was crying and the teardrops made the ink run. But he picks up again . . .

> *She turns the paper over and reads the other side.*

" . . . so now you know the whole story and the reason why. Well she's really laying on that horn now, so. Love, Daddy. PS Look after your sister, you know what she's like."

Sissy, sometimes I know I get short tempered and I'm sorry, because it's not your fault. Daddy asked me to look after you and I have honoured his wish and that meant no going back to Halifax, no Home Ec degree for me, no picking up again with Mike Dunaga—not that I would, but—you know what I mean. I had to make sacrifices to stay here but I don't want you to feel bad—you don't owe me nothin'.

SISSY: Ah thanks, Yewina, but—

YEW: No! No need for thank yous. You are what you are. I made my choices. We can't have everything in life.

SISSY: But maybe we—

YEW: No we can't. But I do have the satisfaction of knowing I've done my duty.

SISSY: Are you sure that you—

YEW: I'm sure. I would never let you be abando—aban—left twice.

SISSY: Because—

YEW: It's okay. You don't have to say anyth—

SISSY: 'Cause I thought that letter was to me.

YEW: Wha'?

SISSY: I thought that letter was to me.

YEW: To wha'?

SISSY: I'm pretty sure Daddy left that for me. That he told me to look after you.

YEW: Ahhh ... are you outta your mind? Why would he want you to look after me?

SISSY: Well, Yewina. You're not very good with people.

YEW: I'm plenty good, thank you.

SISSY: You don't even talk to the chickens.

YEW: Of course not.

SISSY: And you only ever had one real friend, Ethel and she's gone now and it's a hard row to hoe on your own when you're ... like you are.

> *YEW is puzzled.*

Like Marcella ...

> *Pause.*

YEW: Albino?

SISSY: Scared of being alone.

YEW: What!! Oh my god—you—YOU—you thought you were taking care of me? And how did you find out about the letter? How could you think it was to you? How?

SISSY: I found it on our dresser. I guess I musta left it on your bed after I read it—but it makes sense. Daddy had to look after Mom and I had to look after you.

YEW: Ah whoah, okay. Mom was a sleepwalking, plate-smashing, hair-chopping, lunatic banshee. I mean, I loved her—but, come on! You think I!? I need to be taken care of by you? What can you possibly do that I don't??

SISSY: Lots.

YEW: Lots?

SISSY: You . . . never pick fresh flowers for the table—

YEW: Because that's not important!

SISSY: Yewina! I will pretend I didn't hear that.

YEW: You leave the kettle on and wander off leavin' the door flappin' wide open. You don't have a clue, you tell those damn stories over and over . . .

SISSY: I thought you like stories.

YEW: That's not the point. The point is— You. You have no clue how life works. You couldn't shoot a rabbit.

SISSY: But I don't have to because Dan is a bad driver and he hits them with . . . his—oh. Oh, Yewina!

YEW: Yeah, Sissy, that's right. I've been bringing home the meat because I know how to hunt and you wouldn't even if you could. You live on stories and, and dewdrops! You'd let the squirrels and the spiders run the place. You're, you're different!

SISSY: I am difdrent because I didn't think it was a sacrifice to stay and look after you—that is, when I thought that that was what I was supposed to be doing. But you did make sacrifices and stayed because you didn't want to see me abrandaned again.

YEW: ABANDONED!! Abandoned! Why can't you say that? Abandoned! Abandoned! You're abandoned! I'm abandoned! They abandoned us!!! Abandamus, abandatis, abandant, yabbadabbadoodan-bandoned! ABANDONED! Abandoned! Abandoned . . . abandoned.

SISSY: You're not happy.

YEW: It's not about being happy.

SISSY: I think it is . . .

> *SISSY gets the money from the SUGAR bowl.*

You should go—go finish your Home Eggonomics degree—

YEW: Get real.

SISSY: —or go visit Ethel in Paris. Go.

YEW: Hey, hey, that's the Rainy Day Fund.

SISSY: So what? Maybe it's raining in Paris. Go. Take off. I don't want you here if you're not happy.

YEW: Don't be stupid, put that / back.

SISSY: / I'm fine here by myself.

YEW: / Bullshit.

SISSY: / Go do what you want.

YEW: It doesn't matter / what I want.

SISSY: / Yes it does. What do you want?

YEW: I want you to stop / being ridiculous.

SISSY: / What do you want?

YEW: / Stop it.

SISSY: / What do you want?

YEW: I want to be here!

SISSY: Here?

YEW: Here. I like setting on the porch shooting cans—'cause, you know— "When there's nothing to do." —ho boys I'll do it—although I suppose I could get a coupla Jerrys out to help me roof the barn—

SISSY: Yeah!

YEW: But other than that—well, and I s'pose we could have the hippies out for supper—

SISSY: Eee!

YEW: —and maybe get a dog.

SISSY: Aw!

YEW: —and yes maybe I would like to go to Paris for Christmas.

SISSY: Do it! I'll look after Sandy Webster.

YEW: Who's Sandy Webster?

SISSY: Your dog.

YEW: ... Right. Anyway. I would like to see Ethel. I could maybe help out in the restaurant—

SISSY: And meet Edwin and Dorothy's twins!

YEW: Wow, Ethel's an aunt. Auntie Ethel.

SISSY: And Auntie Yewina.

YEW: *(chuckling)* Yeah, but just for a visit though.

SISSY: Or a buncha visits.

YEW: Could be. We'll see, but look—I'm happy here too. With you.

SISSY: Me too.

YEW: Sorry about Scott.

SISSY: Oh, I'll always be with him. He has my caul.

YEW: He took off with your caul? Little bast—

SISSY: I gave it to him.

YEW: Wha'?

SISSY: I crumbled it into little pieces and boiled it up in the coffee.

YEW: You put it in the coffee?

SISSY: It dissolved pretty good.

YEW: Ew, Sissy, you don't know if that was safe to do.

SISSY: It was just like making regular coffee only now with more caul.

YEW: No, I mean, who knows what crap and bugs are in an old caul.

SISSY: There were a coupla chunky lumps—

YEW: Oh god.

SISSY: —I had to smoosh 'em with the spoon against the side of the pot. It will protect him now and we'll always be connected.

YEW: I drank that coffee.

SISSY: He gave me his man seed and I gave him my caul. Pretty fair, doncha think?

YEW: Oh god.

YEW runs to barf in the sink.

SISSY: Are you okay, 'Weena?

YEW: Gaaahk!

SISSY: Oh, Yewina, come on, you shoot bunnies and you're afraid of a little caul? Pshaw!

YEW's head is between her knees, recovering.

YEW: Oh my god!! Why, why, why do you do the things you do!? Oh, my guts. I can feel it just setting in there.

SISSY: Well that's good then, see you're protected too now!

YEW: Oh god, oh god. I don't understand this is the worst day of our lives since Daddy and Mom abandoned us and you're not even upset.

SISSY: Because I found something . . .

SISSY reaches into her bra and takes out eggs.

Look, Yewina!

YEW: Is it something else disgusting?

SISSY: No, something wonderful.

YEW: I don't trust your idea of wonderful, just tell me.

SISSY: It's Sheila's children.

YEW lifts her head. SISSY is holding the eggs in front of YEW's face.

That's why she was trying to get to the apple tree! It wasn't just to get away from the coggar, it was to protect her eggs.

YEW: Oh my god. Are they . . . ali—?

SISSY: Yup, they're warm. Feel them.

She touches an egg to YEW's cheek.

Can you feel that? Fertile . . . There! Feel her moving in the shell?

YEW: Ahuh.

SISSY: When I laid Sheila and John Arthur down, I saw the eggs in the crotch of the apple tree. Sheila was brooding her nest there. Here, Yewina.

She puts an egg in YEW's hand and motions for her to put the egg down her shirt. Stunned, YEW complies.

There now. We will brood these eggs and these eggs will have eggs, will have eggs, will have eggs . . . and we will always have eggs . . .

The sisters each hold an egg under their shirts against their hearts. YEW *reaches out and takes* SISSY'S *hand.*

YEW: Yup, yes we will, Sissy. And we will have each other.

SISSY: Yup. And eggs.

YEW: And . . . each other . . .

SISSY: And eggs.

YEW: . . . And eggs.

SISSY: . . . And each other.

YEW: Yup.

SISSY: Yup. . . and eggs.

Acta est fabula.

Thank Yous!!!

Thank you to Arts Nova Scotia and the Canada Council for the Arts, Chris Chisholm and Goober, Christian Murray, Jeremy Webb, Emlyn Murray, Margaret Smith, Ryanne Chisholm, Heidi Malazdrewich, and fellow Lunabella Martha Irving.

Mary-Colin Chisholm has written or co-written a dozen plays and more sketches than she can shake a shtick at. Her plays have had multiple productions across the country. Recent work includes *Shadows in the Cove: The Notorious Life and Calamitous End of Dr. Henry Inch*, *A Belly Full* (with Marcia Kash), *By the Dark of the Moon* (with Christian Murray), *To Capture Light*, and *He'd Be Your Father's Mother's Cousin*. Whenever she can she lives in a shack by the sea in Jimtown, Nova Scotia, where there's nothing to do and she's more than happy to do it.